DORA

A guide to the EU Digital Operational Resilience Act

DORA

A guide to the EU Digital Operational Resilience Act

ANDREW PATTISON

IT Governance Publishing

Every possible effort has been made to ensure that the information contained in this book is accurate at the time of going to press, and the publisher and the author cannot accept responsibility for any errors or omissions, however caused. Any opinions expressed in this book are those of the author, not the publisher. Websites identified are for reference only, not endorsement, and any website visits are at the reader's own risk. No responsibility for loss or damage occasioned to any person acting, or refraining from action, as a result of the material in this publication can be accepted by the publisher or the author.

Apart from any fair dealing for the purposes of research or private study, or criticism or review, as permitted under the Copyright, Designs and Patents Act 1988, this publication may only be reproduced, stored or transmitted, in any form, or by any means, with the prior permission in writing of the publisher or, in the case of reprographic reproduction, in accordance with the terms of licences issued by the Copyright Licensing Agency. Enquiries concerning reproduction outside those terms should be sent to the publisher at the following address:

IT Governance Publishing Ltd
Unit 3, Clive Court
Bartholomew's Walk
Cambridgeshire Business Park
Ely, Cambridgeshire
CB7 4EA
United Kingdom
www.itgovernancepublishing.co.uk

© Andrew Pattison, 2024.

The author has asserted the rights of the author under the Copyright, Designs and Patents Act, 1988, to be identified as the author of this work.

First edition published in the United Kingdom in 2024 by IT Governance Publishing.

ISBN 978-1-78778-451-2

Cover image originally sourced from Shutterstock®.

ABOUT THE AUTHOR

Andrew Pattison is the Head of GRC consultancy at IT Governance Europe. He has been working in information security, risk management and business continuity since the mid-1990s, helping multiple large international organisations across many sectors. Andrew is a certified auditor, as well as holding CISM and CRISC certifications. He has provided extensive training in multiple GRC fields and is an approved APMG trainer.

CONTENTS

Chapter 1: Introduction 1
   A summary of DORA 4
   Key definitions 11
Chapter 2: An overall approach to compliance 17
   Identify gaps 18
   Risk management 20
   Supply chain 21
Chapter 3: Implementation process 25
   Pre-project 25
   Project mandate 26
   Project initiation 28
   Project initiation 34
   Framework initiation 39
   Measurement, monitoring and review 40
   Audit 42
   Continual improvement 43
Chapter 4: Governance 45
   Terms of reference 49
Chapter 5: Risk management 53
   Risk management framework 56
Chapter 6: Incident response and reporting 67
Chapter 7: Digital operational resilience testing 77
   Testing of ICT tools and systems 80
   Threat-led penetration testing 81
Chapter 8: ICT third-party risk management 87
   Requirements for use of third parties 89
   Oversight of critical third-party service providers 99

Contents

Chapter 9: Information and intelligence sharing 101
Further reading 103

CHAPTER 1: INTRODUCTION

For organisations operating in the financial sector, government interference and regulatory oversight are nothing new. It stands to reason, of course: finances dictate so much of how a country and society functions that the power of government could be hobbled should the financial sector be struck down or left impotent. Furthermore, a secure financial market draws business to itself, which is obviously desirable for all governments.

Through the centuries, the specific threats to finance have changed here and there in the detail, but they typically include market volatility, credit risks, operational risks and actions by outsiders (whether military threats to the nation or otherwise). Organisations in the finance sector have had centuries to understand these threats and have, more or less, settled how to manage them while ensuring enough agility to take advantage of key opportunities and without getting too bogged down in red tape. Risk does, after all, often present opportunities.

In the twentieth century, as businesses in general migrated to digital environments, financial organisations were among the earliest adopters. No small amount of money was spent ensuring that cash and investments were protected from both deliberate and accidental harm in this new digital format. But, of course, the technology kept evolving.

In the twenty-first century, technology has saturated nearly every aspect of doing business, and so the ability to protect

1: Introduction

information – and the systems that access that information – has become paramount. This extends, obviously, to the need to ensure that these systems and information remain accessible and usable during a crisis.

Cyber security – the broad discipline of protecting digital information and systems – is only one part of the rubric, although it is the obvious starting point. What organisations must now implement is resilience: the ability to survive and persist despite forces acting in opposition, whether human, manmade or natural disasters. This represents an elasticity that enables the organisation to spring back into shape.

Targeted cyber attacks, which often take the form of strategic offensives driven by malicious actors with specific objectives, can have an enduring impact. They can persist within systems for extended periods, forcing the organisation to operate at a diminished capacity, or delete or corrupt data and interfere with systems. For these reasons, they pose an ongoing threat to the organisation's ability to function.

Other indiscriminate cyber attacks are also a persistent threat. Although the majority of these may be seen off with basic defences, larger attacks with an infectious component may have particularly significant impact, as exemplified by the infamous WannaCry ransomware. Such events underscore the need for resilience and the ability to swiftly restore normalcy.

For financial entities, which – as noted – are a critical component of a country's wellbeing, nation-state actions can also present a significant threat. In these cases, financial organisations find themselves pawns in geopolitical conflicts.

1: Introduction

Beyond the digital realm, the data and systems that financial institutions rely on may be vulnerable to both manmade and natural disasters, such as fires, floods or prolonged power outages. These, again, present a threat to digital operational resilience.

Digital operational resilience encompasses the capacity to endure and adapt to a wide array of incidents, ranging from meticulously planned cyber attacks to the unpredictable wrath of nature.

Given the increasing numbers and capabilities of cyber threats – not to mention the many ways that the physical world can threaten the digital – and the importance of the financial sector to the correct functioning of the state, it is reasonable and predictable that laws and regulations would follow.

In 2016, the Directive on security of network and information systems (NIS Directive) required EU member states to implement frameworks for securing critical infrastructure. This was largely focused on the threats posed to the information systems on which infrastructure relies, but was fairly broad as it needed to be applied to a range of industries and across the EU. As is common with directives, however, this resulted in a slow, patchwork application. The new iteration of this directive, NIS 2, aims to provide a clearer standard across the EU, but it remains to be seen how effective this will be, not least because it is, again, a directive, which limits its ability to apply specific measures universally.

In 2020, the European Systemic Risk Board (ESRB) examined systemic cyber risk in the EU financial sector. The resulting report found that the primary risks arose from

1: Introduction

key developments in modern networks and ways of doing business[1]:

1. High levels of interconnectedness across financial entities and markets.
2. Interdependence between systems – e.g. payments systems, securities clearing and settlement, claims management, peer-to-peer finance, etc.
3. Deepened interconnectedness between financial entities and third-party service providers and suppliers.
4. Financial entities deploy services across national borders and cyber threats know no borders.
5. Likelihood that vulnerabilities can propagate across the entire EU financial system, compromising stability of EU financial systems.

It was a combination of these factors that led the EU to create DORA, the Digital Operational Resilience Act.

A summary of DORA

Regulation, not directive

From a legislative perspective, the key thing to know about DORA is that it is a regulation. Under EU law, there are two primary types of legislation: directives and regulations. A directive sets out parameters and objectives for EU member states to implement laws. That is, a directive

---

[1] ESRB, *Systemic cyber risk*, February 2020, *https://www.esrb.europa.eu/pub/pdf/reports/esrb.report200219_systemiccyberrisk~101a09685e.en.pdf*.

1: Introduction

instructs the member states to pass laws to achieve a certain objective. As such, directives often result in differing requirements depending on where you are.

A regulation, meanwhile, acts as primary legislation in each member state without needing to be passed into law separately by each country. This also means that requirements are consistent across the EU. Many member states will go on to pass laws to formalise this in domestic law and to include additional requirements relevant to the country's environment and needs.

So, as a regulation, DORA will be enforced from a fixed date regardless of what any member state does. Some countries may apply more restrictive conditions, but it is not possible for any of them to override DORA to relax requirements.

It is important to note, however, that the law as written is not complete: the regulation sets out a number of areas where key authorities must develop the specific detail of the requirements. At the time of writing, these technical standards are yet to be completed, but they will comprise an important part of complying with the law.

Interaction with NIS 2

While there is clearly a lot of overlap with NIS 2, Article 4 of that directive notes that the NIS requirements do not apply to entities that fall under sector-specific legislation such as DORA.[2] This means that for most organisations in

---

[2] Directive on measures for a high common level of cybersecurity across the Union (NIS 2 Directive), Article 4(1).

1: Introduction

the financial sector, there is only one compliance framework for operational resilience to follow. Given that DORA applies a number of exemptions, however, it is possible that some organisations that remain exempt from DORA compliance may still fall under NIS 2's remit.

Key roles under DORA

Financial entities are, obviously, organisations involved in the finance sector. The Regulation provides a comprehensive list of the organisations that are bound by DORA in Article 2(1). It is important to note that this list includes "ICT third-party service providers", but these are not included in what are considered "financial entities". This is addressed – albeit briefly – in the clause following this list, which explains that *"For the purposes of this Regulation, entities referred to in paragraph 1, points (a) to (t), shall collectively be referred to as 'financial entities'."*[3]

Article 2(3) goes on to provide explicit exclusions from the law.

ICT third-party suppliers are defined in Article 4(19) as *"an undertaking providing ICT services", which is obviously brief and terrifyingly broad, but for the purposes of the Regulation should be read as "an undertaking providing ICT services [to organisations identified as financial entities or within the supply chain for organisations identified as financial entities]"*.

---

[3] DORA, Article 2(2).

1: Introduction

Competent authorities, like supervisory authorities and competent authorities established in other EU legislation, are bodies that each member state nominates to oversee compliance with DORA. Unlike many other laws, however, DORA recognises the variety of organisations in the finance sector, and Article 46 sets out how each competent authority should be identified.

European Supervisory Authorities (ESAs) are collectively the EU's authority on how the Regulation should be applied. The three ESAs are the European Banking Authority (EBA), European Insurance and Occupational Pensions Authority (EIOPA) and European Securities and Markets Authority (ESMA). They are responsible for developing the technical standards that flesh out the specific detail of DORA compliance. It may be useful to note that the Regulation may be seen as more agile than other laws because it defines so much through these standards, which gives the ESAs the ability to respond to novel threats or shifts in the threat environment without needing to wait for the legislative process to catch up.

Exemptions

DORA repeatedly provides exemptions to various parts of the law – often to microenterprises, which it defines as *"a financial entity, other than a trading venue, a central counterparty, a trade repository or a central securities depository, which employs fewer than 10 persons and has an annual turnover and/or annual balance sheet total that*

1: Introduction

does not exceed EUR 2 million".[4] There are other, more specific exemptions under various articles, so it is important to recognise that the law does not apply consistently across all organisations, or even all organisations within the same field of financial services.

Proportionality principle

One of the more critical elements of DORA is the proportionality principle, which is set out in Article 4. This principle essentially overrides all other requirements set out in the Regulation by allowing organisations to implement the requirements as appropriate to their *"size and overall risk profile, and the nature, scale and complexity of their services, activities and operations"*. It is useful to note that this principle applies differently for Chapter II of the Regulation compared to Chapters III, IV and V. The proportionality principle does not apply to Chapter VI.

While Chapter II may be applied entirely in line with the proportionality principle, the other chapters may apply the principle *"as specifically provided for in the relevant rules"*. That is, the organisation may – relatively freely – interpret an appropriate application for Chapter II, but for the remaining requirements may only follow the permitted variations as set out in the Regulation.

Remember that this is not carte blanche to simply brush aside your obligations or to dilute the work you do to

---

[4] DORA, Article 3(60).

1: Introduction

comply with the law: each competent authority has a duty to consider how each organisation has applied the principle.

It is critical to note that the proportionality principle *solely* addresses financial entities. This means that ICT third parties are not entitled to apply the principle except as directed by the financial entities they serve. Equally, however, it does suggest that financial entities can take their suppliers' needs into account in how they require the supplier to fulfil contractual obligations.

The five pillars

Chapters II to VI set out the 'meat' of the Regulation: the requirements that financial entities and ICT third-party service providers are obliged to meet. These five chapters are essentially the 'pillars' of DORA:

1. ICT risk management
2. ICT-related incident management, classification and reporting
3. Digital operational resilience testing
4. Managing of ICT third-party risk
5. Information-sharing arrangements

The first pillar is the most important, as each of the others draws on it. Risk management is at the heart of the Regulation, and every other part should be viewed through that lens. Usefully, the risk management process will help the organisation correctly apply the proportionality principle.

1: Introduction

Implementation time frame

While DORA came into force on 16 January 2023, it gives organisations time to implement its requirements. The law will apply in full from 17 January 2025. It is possible that some technical standards may not be ready by that date, however, and they likely will be subject to more change than the Regulation itself, so it is best to not consider the state of the law on 17 January 2025 as the final word in digital operational resilience.

Outsourcing operational resilience

It is possible to outsource many of your DORA obligations to third parties. A holistic multi-vendor strategy can be built with outsourced ICT suppliers – but this must be supported by policy and a dependency framework.[5] It is not possible to outsource your accountability for ensuring compliance: your organisation remains accountable for meeting all the applicable DORA requirements, so good governance and oversight of such an outsourcing arrangement is essential.

Creating a mesh of providers to manage the majority of your DORA compliance may be a daunting prospect – especially when most organisations will have the resources in-house to manage many elements of compliance. However, the skills required to verify your compliance may be both less available and more difficult to manage, especially for smaller organisations that find it difficult to appoint independent auditors. As such, it may be valuable to outsource your compliance verification, which passes

---

[5] DORA, Article 6(9).

1: Introduction

the responsibility for confirming compliance to vendors but, again, accountability remains.

For organisations following this route, note that compliance auditors provided by third parties must be competent – which means confirming that the provider's auditors are qualified. Furthermore, the audit plans must be risk prioritised and approved by your organisation, which means you must remain engaged and involved in the process.

Key definitions

Digital operational resilience

"the ability of a financial entity to build, assure and review its operational integrity and reliability by ensuring, either directly or indirectly through the use of services provided by ICT third-party service providers, the full range of ICT-related capabilities needed to address the security of the network and information systems which a financial entity uses, and which support the continued provision of financial services and their quality, including throughout disruptions;"[6]

This is the focus of the Regulation: ensuring that financial entities and their ICT third-party service providers not only secure their information and systems but also demonstrate an ability to continue functioning through disruptions.

---

[6] DORA, Article 3(1).

1: Introduction

ICT risk

> *"any reasonably identifiable circumstance in relation to the use of network and information systems which, if materialised, may compromise the security of the network and information systems, of any technology dependent tool or process, of operations and processes, or of the provision of services by producing adverse effects in the digital or physical environment;"*[7]

Financial entities are generally well versed in risk management, but it is important to ensure that it is addressed in accordance with the Regulation. Much of DORA compliance will, after all, come down to risk management.

ICT-related incident

> *"a single event or a series of linked events unplanned by the financial entity that compromises the security of the network and information systems, and have an adverse impact on the availability, authenticity, integrity or confidentiality of data, or on the services provided by the financial entity;"*[8]

Of particular note here is that, unlike most texts on information security and resilience, DORA also requires organisations to secure the 'authenticity' of information.

---

[7] DORA, Article 3(5).

[8] DORA, Article 3(8).

1: Introduction

Authenticity is about validating the source of information[9]; this sits alongside confidentiality, integrity and availability, ensuring that information is protected and validated.

Major ICT-related incident

> *"an ICT-related incident that has a high adverse impact on the network and information systems that support critical or important functions of the financial entity;"*[10]

The key element of understanding what constitutes a major incident is the impact on critical or important functions.

Critical or important function

> *"a function, the disruption of which would materially impair the financial performance of a financial entity, or the soundness or continuity of its services and activities, or the discontinued, defective or failed performance of that function would materially impair the continuing compliance of a financial entity with the conditions and obligations of its authorisation, or with its other obligations under applicable financial services law;"*[11]

---

[9] NIST SP 800-53 provides a more complete definition: *"The property of being genuine and being able to be verified and trusted; confidence in the validity of a transmission, message, or message originator."*

[10] DORA, Article 3(10).

[11] DORA, Article 3(22).

1: Introduction

As noted above, understanding which of your organisation's activities constitute critical or important functions is at the heart of DORA compliance. Protecting these functions will be the primary focus of the risk management framework.

ICT concentration risk

> *"an exposure to individual or multiple related critical ICT third-party service providers creating a degree of dependency on such providers so that the unavailability, failure or other type of shortfall of such provider may potentially endanger the ability of a financial entity to deliver critical or important functions, or cause it to suffer other types of adverse effects, including large losses, or endanger the financial stability of the Union as a whole;"* [12]

ICT concentration is a significant risk to organisations that rely heavily on third parties. In essence, this is a case of putting too many eggs in one basket – spreading the risk is preferable.

Microenterprise

> *"a financial entity, other than a trading venue, a central counterparty, a trade repository or a central securities depository, which employs fewer than 10 persons and*

---

[12] DORA, Article 3(29)

has an annual turnover and/or annual balance sheet total that does not exceed EUR 2 million;"[13]

Small enterprise

"a financial entity that employs 10 or more persons, but fewer than 50 persons, and has an annual turnover and/or annual balance sheet total that exceeds EUR 2 million, but does not exceed EUR 10 million;"[14]

Medium-sized enterprise

"a financial entity that is not a small enterprise and employs fewer than 250 persons and has an annual turnover that does not exceed EUR 50 million and/or an annual balance sheet that does not exceed EUR 43 million;"[15]

DORA sets out clear bands for organisations of different sizes. This is necessary because microenterprises, for instance, are granted a number of opportunities to reduce their regulatory burden. Equally, as the proportionality principle allows organisations to interpret requirements based on the size of their operation, these are the bands that competent authorities will refer to when assessing whether the organisation has appropriately applied the principle.

---

[13] DORA, Article 3(60).

[14] DORA, Article 3(63).

[15] DORA, Article 3(64).

CHAPTER 2: AN OVERALL APPROACH TO COMPLIANCE

Fundamentally, DORA is about risk management. While you can examine each of the 'pillars' independently, they all come back to this core activity – where you manage your ICT suppliers, you do so on the basis of risk; the way you prepare for incident response is, again, on the basis of risk; and so on.

The finance sector already understands risk – this is a core competence. Furthermore, ICT is not new to the sector, and organisations within it typically understand the risk environment. It is, after all, a rare day that we hear of a bank or credit institution being hit by a major cyber attack.

To build on this, many of DORA's requirements simply reiterate existing expectations from regulators and requirements within the law. For instance, the European Banking Authority's *Guidelines on ICT and security risk management* already sets out many of the same or similar measures outlined in the Regulation. While these are not exact matches in all cases, the similarities give organisations the opportunity to streamline their compliance activities.

As such, implementing DORA compliance should not be a particularly onerous or mentally taxing task. It should, instead, be a matter of simply pivoting existing activities to take a few new details into account.

Of course, what is true for the finance sector is not necessarily true for its service providers, and DORA insists

2: An overall approach to compliance

that these parties have key requirements passed down to them. For many service providers, the requirements will be things they already do, but not as part of a regulatory regime. As such, they may not produce suitable records to demonstrate compliance. Equally, there may be subtle differences between what the Regulation requires and what the service provider does. Ensuring these details are ironed out will be critical to both the financial entities and the service providers. Remember: DORA specifically puts ICT third-party service providers within the scope of the law.

Before getting to the detail of implementing DORA compliance, it is useful to examine how a compliance programme might look from a very high level, while bearing in mind your organisation's role as either a financial entity or an ICT third-party service provider.

Identify gaps

First, organisations should identify and understand where they are failing to meet their compliance obligations. DORA has a large number of very specific requirements, and the technical standards being developed by the ESAs will doubtless introduce even more, so the organisation will need a strong understanding of these requirements.

A gap analysis is a structured assessment of the organisation's operations and processes compared to the desired or ideal state – in this case, DORA compliance. As a process, it helps identify discrepancies, weaknesses and areas of improvement.

The first step – as it is a process of identifying where you stack up against the Regulation's requirements – is to collate all the relevant expectations. Remember that DORA

2: An overall approach to compliance

does not simply apply 'straight out of the box': some types of organisations have differing requirements, and smaller organisations are often exempt from total compliance. Microenterprises, for instance, have a number of points at which they can elect to take simpler approaches.

This means that you will need to pay close attention to the Regulation to ensure that your compliance programme is not wasting time implementing unnecessary measures. It is likely that this list will change as you better understand how DORA applies to you and as the ESAs refine the technical standards.

The organisation can then use this list to consider how its activities and measures align to requirements, identifying gaps and discrepancies. These gaps could manifest in various ways, such as in the use of outdated technology, a lack of skills, inefficient processes, or simply through non-existence.

This process will feed into your risk management, as it produces a clear overview of your current weaknesses, as well as identifying where the Regulation suggests you should be looking for risks. Alongside the actual risk assessment process, the organisation can also be implementing those measures that DORA mandates.

Gaps may, of course, need to be prioritised, and decisions of that sort can be addressed as part of the risk assessment.

Conducting a gap analysis periodically is a good way of ensuring the organisation keeps on top of its obligations, especially if the ESAs change the technical standards. Equally, regulator investigations or court decisions could

2: An overall approach to compliance

affect how the organisation considers the Regulation's requirements.

Risk management

As mentioned, risk management is at the heart of DORA compliance. The organisation will need to establish a strong risk management framework, led from the top of the organisation, to provide real assurance that it can respond appropriately to crises. Your risk management framework is discussed in more detail in Chapter 5 of this book, but much of it can be addressed through existing best-practice risk management standards.

As DORA is fundamentally about information security and resilience, ISO/IEC 27001:2022 is a sensible place to look for guidance on the risk management framework. ISO 27001 provides a structured, systematic approach to identifying, assessing and managing information security risks, and is supported by a set of reference controls that can be applied to address the majority of risks.

Any risk assessment must take into account the organisation's context – that is, the organisation's core functions, the risk environment, key stakeholders and other interested parties, and the scope of the risk assessment. ISO 27001 ensures this is systematically developed as part of the broader information security management activities. The context creates boundaries for the assessment and helps identify the specific risks that should be examined. DORA, obviously, will form a key part of the context, while financial entities and ICT third parties will count each other as stakeholders and interested parties.

2: An overall approach to compliance

ISO 27001 requires the risk management process to produce key documentation, which is not strictly necessary for DORA compliance. However, this documentation is valuable for validating the effectiveness of the organisation's risk management and the process itself. This means that it can be provided to competent authorities as evidence of a good-faith approach to compliance.

ISO 27001 emphasises monitoring and reviewing the risk management process. Like any other major programme, this is necessary because the risk environment is not static – criminals and other threats do not vanish or stop evolving. Furthermore, the process can become prosaic to staff, which risks introducing errors, and processes can become disjointed as they adapt to new conditions. It is not simply reviewing the results of the risk management that is valuable, but the process itself.

All this means that risk management needs to be overseen from the top – financial entities already take financial risk extremely seriously, and information security and resilience risk should be considered the same way. Senior managers and boards need to be informed and included in the programme. This includes allocating resources, setting policies and supporting risk management efforts.

Supply chain

As mentioned, ensuring the supply chain for ICT services also meets its obligations is a separate challenge. While supply chains are typically managed through contracts, which should be reliable ways of ensuring your requirements are met, it is also true that you are relying on a third party to meet **your** legal obligations.

2: An overall approach to compliance

There is an inherent lack of control in these scenarios and, while you might also see that as passing responsibility and accountability to a third party, the law and the regulators are likely to hold the financial entity to account for failures within the supply chain. After all – DORA does require the financial entity to ensure that all ICT third-party service providers comply with the law. If the service provider fails to meet these requirements, this is also a failure on the part of the financial entity.

If your organisation is part of the supply chain, the main difference in your approach to DORA compliance will be that you are able to focus more directly on securing your services than on some of the other requirements in the Regulation. For instance, many of the requirements only apply to financial entities and are not passed on – such as making reports to the competent authorities.

However, a critical part of your role will be to assure the financial entities you work with that your services are indeed secure and resilient. Under DORA, these organisations are required to secure evidence that this is the case, and while some may be happy to accept whatever evidence you provide, it is also likely that some will have specific requirements for what constitutes evidence.

Regardless of whether you are a service provider or a financial entity, you will have a strong interest in how assurance is provided. There are essentially three ways of providing assurance: first party, second party and third party. Each can be described in terms of the effort involved and the assurance provided:

1. **First party**

2: An overall approach to compliance

This usually involves conducting internal audits to check that your processes are in place and effective. This is easy for most organisations and does not involve much disruption. However, it has limited value as assurance for your clients. They are being asked to trust that your audits are fair and accurate.

2. **Second party**

   In this case, the client audits the service provider. This is cheap for the service provider as the cost is borne by the client. It also gives the client a high degree of assurance. However, this can be disruptive as you need to ensure the client's auditors only have access to information and systems necessary for the audit. Furthermore, the assurance is only good for that client. Other clients may wish to also conduct their own audits, which compounds the disruption.

3. **Third party**

   This usually involves seeking certification from an impartial third party. As long as the certification scheme is well regarded and recognised by your clients, the certification alone may be adequate assurance. In some cases, clients may ask for additional information that demonstrates your security in a specific area or using specific technologies. This approach can be costly and time-consuming, but it offers a fairly high degree of assurance and minimises disruption as the organisation is only audited by the certification body.

2: An overall approach to compliance

DORA specifically requires financial entities to ensure that ICT third-party service providers comply with *"appropriate information security standards"*. Furthermore, contracts relating to critical or important functions may only be provided by organisations that use *"the most up-to-date and highest quality information security standards"*.[16] This provides a strong argument for service providers to pursue ISO 27001 certification: not only does this meet the requirement to apply the highest-quality information security standard but it also provides certification as a means of assurance.

---

[16] DORA, Article 28(5).

CHAPTER 3: IMPLEMENTATION PROCESS

Implementing a DORA compliance programme is potentially a large project, especially if you rely heavily on service providers or have little practical experience with information security. Establishing a strong process for the project is crucial, as it will help ensure you address each point in turn and within your organisation's management structures.

This chapter sets out a simple process for ensuring your programme meets DORA's requirements while building a solid structure for ongoing compliance. It is broadly similar to the process we recommend for implementing management systems such as ISO 27001.[17]

Pre-project

Before the project begins, you need to identify and gather key resources. Much of this will simply be research – making sure you have the right people who understand enough about the project to drive it forward.

For many organisations, this will be straightforward but potentially time-consuming. You may well have a

---

[17] For a more detailed explanation of this process, see Alan Calder's *Nine Steps to Success: An ISO 27001:2013 Implementation Overview*, https://www.itgovernancepublishing.co.uk/product/nine-steps-to-success.

3: Implementation process

compliance manager, for instance, but they need to develop a stronger understanding of DORA.

This is also the stage at which you might conduct a gap analysis (see previous chapter). This provides a valuable information base for the project to proceed. As the next stage involves getting support and approval for the project from senior management, a gap analysis will help you determine the time and other resource costs involved in achieving compliance.

Project mandate

No project can reasonably hope to succeed unless it is approved and overseen by senior management. For compliance projects, this is especially true. Senior management has a clear interest in ensuring the organisation meets its legal and regulatory obligations, and in some jurisdictions may be personally liable for compliance.

From the start of the project, you will need a project leader who takes the initiative and begins the push for DORA compliance. Everyone else in the organisation who needs to know about the project or operational resilience will look to this person for information and guidance.

The project leader has a tough job: they need to be able to reduce something that may look complex, difficult and expensive to something that everyone believes can be achieved – and, crucially, they need to believe that it can be achieved in the time frame allocated and with the resources allowed. And then, of course, the project leader has to make it all happen!

3: Implementation process

For all this to work, the project leader needs to set up the project in such a way that it is adequately resourced, that there is enough time – including allowing time for things that might go wrong – and that everyone understands the project risks. They also need to ensure there are controls in place to manage these risks to the project and make sure all the relevant parties apply them.

What is absolutely critical is support from the top of the organisation. At an early stage, this is potentially more important than having a full understanding of what the project will entail. Operational resilience is both a management and a governance issue. Successfully implementing DORA compliance, therefore, is utterly reliant on the project having real support from the top of the organisation. This is fundamentally binary: without support, there is little to no chance of success; with support, it is entirely manageable. This support needs to be authentic – simple lip service or occasional discussions will not suffice.

Just as you need a single project leader, you need a central project sponsor at the top of the organisation. This is not necessarily the CEO or a director, but it does need to be someone capable of being accountable for the project's success or failure.

With a project leader and project sponsor, you can produce the project mandate, which is essentially a documented set of answers to the questions all projects face in their early stages:

- What are we hoping to achieve?
- How long will the project take?

3: Implementation process

- What resources will the project require, both financially and otherwise?
- Does the project have top management support?

The answers establish the project objectives and give senior management the information they need to approve the project and keep track of it as it develops. Developing these answers may involve a lot of research and preparation – gap analyses, budgeting, reviewing case studies, and so on – but is time well spent.

The project mandate is something you can come back to as the project develops as a sort of high-level overview of what it is you are trying to achieve and the process for doing so. It is not a blow-by-blow project plan, but it is a useful litmus test for making sure you are staying on track and on target.

It does, of course, need to be approved by senior management – this is the 'mandate' part of the name. It is documented proof that the top of the organisation has approved the project and of what exactly they have approved. For this reason, you need to make sure it is broadly realistic. Almost everyone has seen what happens to projects that overrun or lose their way, and it is not desirable to be one of the people in charge of those projects. By having top management approve your mandate, you are tying your professional reputation to the project!

Project initiation

With the project mandate in place, it is time to set up the project itself and the project governance structure. This is effectively an extension of what is in the project mandate,

3: Implementation process

building it out into a practical document or set of documents.

The project governance structure will consist of:

- The project objective;
- The project team, with a project board if you expect the project to be lengthy or problematic;
- A project plan, including scheduled review dates; and
- A project risk register.

Objectives

The project objectives and operational resilience objectives will feed into the key, top-level policy documents and will inform your requirements around monitoring, measurement, analysis and evaluation, and management review. These objectives should include a time-bound statement regarding compliance with DORA in addition to the key information security and resilience objectives. If you intend to use ISO 27001 certification as assurance of aspects of your DORA compliance, you should also include the certification timeline in your time-bound objective.

Project team

Larger organisations might find it useful or suitable to have a two-level management structure for the project team: a management steering group and an executive project team. The steering group would be responsible for the high-level approach, including strategy, project governance and oversight. The executive team would be responsible for the operational approach, including designing, implementing and operating the compliance programme.

3: Implementation process

Smaller organisations, meanwhile, are unlikely to have the manpower necessary for a split function, nor are they likely to be complex enough to need such a structure. In this case, the functions of both groups should be fulfilled by a single project team.

This project team should be drawn from those parts of the organisation most likely to be affected by the compliance project. While there will obviously be a strong IT element, the team should also recognise the critical and important functions that DORA demands you protect. After all, the measures that need to be put in place to create operational resilience will affect those who have to work with them potentially much more significantly than those who have to put the measures in place.

The balance is important: a properly functioning resilience programme will depend on everyone in the organisation understanding and applying its controls. If the project team is balanced in favour of non-technical people, it is more likely to produce something that everyone in the organisation understands and can apply.

The change process for operational resilience may have a cultural impact. As such, those who can best represent and articulate the needs and concerns of their parts of the organisation should be selected for the project team. Without their involvement, there is unlikely to be the buy-in necessary for the project to be effectively developed and implemented.

Project team members should be in senior positions across the organisation and representing a good mix of disciplines. Key functions that should be represented are quality/process management, human resources, training,

3: Implementation process

and IT and facilities management. Of course, operational resilience has a strong information security component, so there will need to be involvement from the manager responsible for information security and a trained information security expert. In terms of functions that should also be represented, among the most critical will be sales, operations and administration. People in these roles will be most affected by implementing operational resilience, so should have strong voices in the project.

For hopefully obvious reasons, the team should include an experienced project manager to keep track of the project and report progress against the planned objectives. This reporting should be directly to either the chair of the steering group or to the project sponsor.

Project plan

A structured approach to the implementation should sit behind your project plan. The following elements should all be addressed as you build this out:

- A continual improvement model, such as PDCA (Plan, Do, Check, Act) or similar.
- Your approach to documentation, including how policies create functional procedures, which produce records that demonstrate compliance.
- The management framework, including the internal and external context of the organisation.
- The scope of the project.

3: Implementation process

- Key policies, with allocated roles and responsibilities – including the role responsible for reporting on the performance of the compliance programme.
- A systematic approach to risk assessment and the risk acceptance criteria.
- How you will identify and evaluate options for the treatment of risks.
- How you will document the results of risk assessment and treatment so that it can be tracked and measured.
- The implementation of risk treatments and controls.
- Appropriate training for affected staff, as well as staff awareness programmes.
- How the programme will be managed and resourced following the implementation project.
- Procedures for monitoring, reviewing, testing and audit.
- Procedures for reviewing the programme and the outcomes of testing and audits in light of a changing risk environment, new technology or other circumstances.
- How improvements to the compliance programme should be identified, documented and implemented.

In larger or complex organisations, it may be a more sensible approach to split the overall project into several project plans, dividing it in line with the clearly separable parts of the organisation. This can reduce the complexity of the project and allow each part to take an individually phased approach in line with its needs.

3: Implementation process

There is a further potential benefit to splitting up the project in this way: leveraging expertise. Where you are able to clearly differentiate the scope between two different parts of the organisation, it may be possible to gain a great deal of experience designing and implementing the compliance project. If this is accompanied by a track record of success and the momentum from that success, it is possible to use that to roll out the programme across the rest of the organisation quickly and effectively.

While there can be significant benefits to this approach, they will all be lost if the scoping simply creates 'artificial' business units. You must be very clear that each implementation area is a truly distinct entity, otherwise you run the risk that one function is being pulled towards compliance by the elements of the business that have started implementation while being held back by another that has not yet begun.

The plan should be prepared by the project team and match the key steps in the high-level timeline set out in the project mandate. Once it has been assessed by the CEO and top management, it should then be approved by the board. This plan must be understood by senior management and the board from their perspectives: it should reflect what was established in the mandate in terms of costs and effort. It should also provide enough space for those who will have to implement the plan to find appropriate solutions to challenges that may materialise. In short, the plan should be detailed enough to be useful and flexible enough to adapt to the circumstances.

3: Implementation process

Risk register

When starting the project, the team should identify risks to the success of the project. These often arise from internal issues, such as weak management commitment, inadequate resourcing, competition for resources and time, inertia or resistance to change, the need for cultural change, and so on. Other risks may result from external issues, such as client timelines, conflicting or competing regulations, and so on.

Your risk register should collate all of these risks. Just as for any other risk management process, each risk should have an owner, and there should be identified measures to mitigate those risks. The project team should regularly review the risk register and progress on mitigating the risks. This can make a substantial difference to the implementation of the project plan.

Project initiation

Project initiation is about establishing the 'norms' of the project: those things that will be consistent across the project and act as a kind of frame for the whole thing. This encompasses continual improvement processes, establishing responsibilities and relationships, and documentation.

It is important to get these right before you start implementing DORA's specific requirements, because it ensures that all your measures operate within the same framework and under the same conditions.

3: Implementation process

Continual improvement

Your project plan should already have established the continual improvement framework that you intend to use for your operation resilience programme. There are many approaches to continual improvement, and often organisations will already have a preferred model, such as the ITIL® 7 Step Continual Service Improvement approach, the COBIT® Continual Improvement Life Cycle, or PDCA, as mentioned earlier.

Whichever continual improvement model your organisation uses, the project team should understand it before work starts so that it can inform each of the following steps. After all, it is quite likely that the project will have some elements start to function before others are complete, and those will need to be corrected or improved before the project as a whole has concluded.

It is also important to remember that continual improvement, as the name suggests, is not just for errors, but also to recognise where improvements can be made and efficiencies can be applied. To take advantage of this, the organisation should encourage engagement from all levels.

The continual improvement process should also include root-cause analysis. This will help the organisation identify whether similar issues may affect other elements in the project – or later arise. This will be especially valuable where the programme needs to be applied in stages across the organisation, as it allows the project team to save time in later stages by avoiding known issues. Once the programme is up and running, it will also help the organisation quickly stamp out vulnerabilities and inefficiencies.

3: Implementation process

Responsibilities and relationships

Any significant programme will need to establish a RACI matrix, which tracks who is responsible, accountable, consulted and informed on various aspects. In particular, responsibility and accountability will be identified early – these are the people, or roles, who will take ownership for each part of the implementation and management of the processes.

The roles that need to be identified are those who will be responsible and accountable for the following:

- Oversight of the establishment, implementation, operation, maintenance and improvement of the operational resilience programme.
- Continual improvement.
- Risk management framework.
- Incident management.
- Supply chain management.

The RACI matrix obviously also needs to identify who should be consulted and informed, but these people or roles can be identified almost on the fly as these core elements are developed.

Documentation

Documentation is necessarily a time-consuming part of any project. It can be more onerous if you have not planned how your documentation will be structured or do not have an organisation-wide standard for developing each document. Equally, it can be a relatively straightforward process if your organisation already has a streamlined process and

3: Implementation process

effective templates. Having a documentation specialist such as a technical writer can be especially valuable to ensure your documentation is concise, effective and cleverly organised.

Documentation must be complete, comprehensive and in line with the relevant requirements (DORA, in this case), and fit your organisation like a glove. DORA does not set out exactly what must be documented, so the organisation must determine for itself what is necessary and what is not. This can be made simpler if you take the approach of applying ISO management systems such as ISO 27001 and ISO 22301, which dictate to some degree what must be documented.[18]

If you are driving your own documentation, it is helpful to understand the sorts of information you should think about documenting. Your risk management framework, for instance, will define your risk management processes, which determine the controls that you must deploy. Each of those controls and the processes that identify them should be documented. You will also produce records of your activities – such as the results of the risk assessment – which are valuable information demonstrating that you are

---

[18] For a more detailed explanation of ISO 22301, see Alan Calder's *ISO 22301:2019 and business continuity management – Understand how to plan, implement and enhance a business continuity management system (BCMS)*,
https://www.itgovernance.co.uk/shop/product/iso-223012019-and-business-continuity-management-understand-how-to-plan-implement-and-enhance-a-business-continuity-management-system-bcms.

3: Implementation process

fulfilling your obligations and following the correct processes. Without this level of documentation, it is not possible to really apply continual improvement – after all, how can you find inefficiencies in a process that is not documented? You might intuit that certain things could be improved and stumble your way into making improvements, but that is not the basis for an effective process.

Documentation should be adequate but not excessive. It is very easy to create processes and procedures for every little thing that must be completed, but this creates blinkered thinking and discourages innovation. It can also be a nightmare to maintain.

There are some key documents, however, that will be necessary:

- The top-level information security and continuity policies, the risk assessment procedure, the risk treatment plan and the scope of the project. Retaining the minutes of board and steering committee meetings endorsing the project and its scope may also be valuable.
- The procedures that implement specific controls, which will be identified by your risk assessment procedure. There is likely to be one such procedure for each of the selected controls.
- Documents that deal with how the ISMS is monitored, reviewed and continually improved, including measuring progress towards the information security objectives.

3: Implementation process

Documentation is only as good as the procedures that control it. Simply having a folder full of procedures and policies but no way of knowing who has amended them, when and for what reason renders the documents of dubious value. We need to be able to trust that the documents are an accurate reflection of what the organisation intends to achieve. As such, you need to consider how documents are developed, maintained, amended and retired. How does a user know that the version of the document they are reading is the current one? Who is responsible for maintaining it and who for approving any changes?

Given the nature of the project, there will be a number of documents that need to be subject to strict security measures. These will include the risk assessment and the risk treatment plan, as well as information about how the organisation manages various aspects of security. These documents should be classified, restricted and treated in accordance with the organisation's information classification system.

Framework initiation

This part of the process involves implementing all the specific measures – those that are required by the Regulation. This is by far the largest part of the process, simply because it involves getting down into the nitty gritty. We will discuss each of the sections in more detail in the following chapters.

3: Implementation process

Measurement, monitoring and review

While establishing measures to comply with DORA may feel like the conclusion of the process, in reality you are merely halfway. Having built all your new processes and negotiated with relevant parties to secure information and systems, you might have created something that complies with DORA *for now*. Over time, processes slip, people become lazy, new vulnerabilities arise, software gets patched, and so on.

You need to take a long-term view. This means that you need to measure the effectiveness of the overall programme, not just the processes and controls that you adopt to meet your compliance requirements. While those processes and controls are the measures that keep regulators happy, the wider policies and processes are what keep the programme functioning.

Furthermore, until you check the effectiveness of your measures, you do not know if they are working as intended – it is entirely possible that you have created an edifice that looks nice from the outside but serves no real purpose. You need to confirm that your work is meeting the objectives you have set for it.

Clearly, operational resilience needs to be measured against performance targets in just the same way as other parts of the organisation, which ties back into the objectives you identified in the project mandate and built out during project initiation.

To develop a useful set of metrics, you need to determine what exactly you are measuring, how you will measure it and how often it needs to be measured. This should all be

3: Implementation process

documented so you have a point of reference, which can be updated as better ways of measuring your processes are identified.

Many measurements can be automated – logs of system notifications, for instance – while others must be conducted manually. It is important to automate as much of this as possible, however, as manual measures may suffer from subjective assessments that may show differences depending on who takes the measurement.

There are some key areas that contribute to the success of the programme and its objectives, and should be carefully examined to assess their effectiveness:

- Controls and groups of controls selected to address the most significant risks identified in the risk assessment.
- Information security and continuity awareness, education and training.
- Vulnerability patching and management.
- The incident handling process.
- Perimeter security.
- Penetration testing.

By implementing an effective monitoring, measuring and corrective action regime alongside a formal review process, you can start driving the continual improvement that you established at the start of the project.

Top management should review the compliance programme's performance at least annually. These reviews should look at a summary of the measurements – such as where they demonstrate a failure to meet objectives – the results of audits (see the next section), and improvement activities resulting from previous reviews.

3: Implementation process

The management review should look at the compliance programme both internally and externally. Internal considerations relate to the programme's performance in relation to its objectives. Externally, the review should consider the world in which the organisation operates to ensure it is taking appropriate steps to respond to changes in its operating and risk environment.

Audit

Your compliance programme has to work in the real world; the people in the organisation must be applying the processes correctly and following policy to make sure you meet your legal obligations.

Auditing is a crucial assessment of your efforts. While measurements and checks look at how effective your measures are, the audit also checks that your plans and processes are being applied as intended. Just like other audits that are common in the financial sector, you are examining conformity, not just effectiveness. If certain processes are not being followed as described, why is that? Are they too onerous? Too technical and confusing to the users? Are they inefficient? Have users been appropriately trained to follow them? Measurements may not capture this at all.

For organisations without a great deal of auditing experience, ISO 19011:2018 is a good place to start. This is an international standard that focuses on editing management systems; typically those based on other ISO management system standards. However, the principles of auditing are consistent, and the overall structures you put in place to manage DORA compliance will be a form of

3: Implementation process

management system, even if you do not take a strict ISO approach to compliance (such as by implementing ISO 27001 and ISO 22301).

Audits can be conducted across the whole programme, but it is not usually necessary to cover the whole programme at once. Instead, you might split it up into audits that take place a few months apart so that, over a year, you audit every part of the programme.

As part of your project, you will need to build a team of trained internal auditors. These auditors can be drawn from around the organisation and, just like other audits, should never audit any part of the business for which they – or their managers – are responsible.

The results of audits should be fed into the management reviews described in the previous section.

Continual improvement

Continual improvement gets mentioned a lot, as you might have noticed. This is not because the law requires it or because we are fanatical about operational resilience. Rather, it is the sensible way to approach any regime that is intended to function in the long term.

Once you have a functioning set of processes, which you measure and audit, passing the results to management review, you have all the data you need to start improving things. An improvement might be a simple thing, such as streamlining a procedure or reassigning responsibility for something. Or it might be a larger project in itself to improve the overall framework in which your compliance programme operates. The important thing is to recognise

3: Implementation process

that improvements do not necessarily end: you should never assume that a process is 'perfect', no matter how effective it is. Your management reviews should remain curious so that any relevant improvement can be proposed, assessed and, if it seems promising, implemented and later reviewed.

CHAPTER 4: GOVERNANCE

One of the first requirements set out in DORA is that financial entities must establish *"an internal governance and control framework"* for overseeing the organisation's risk management activities.[19] While the Regulation's requirements in relation to this are relatively slim – taking up on a single article – this is potentially one of the most important parts of DORA compliance.

The management body that the Regulation sets out will be necessary to ensure compliance with DORA's other requirements, and – of special note – has the *"ultimate responsibility for managing the financial entity's ICT risk"*.[20] This is no small duty, as you can imagine.

As with most governance roles, the management body will be primarily involved at the policy and strategy level. DORA sets out the specific governance duties of the management body[21]:

a) Be responsible for managing ICT risk.
b) Establish policies to preserve the confidentiality, integrity, availability and authenticity of data.

---

[19] DORA, Article 5(1).

[20] DORA, Article 5(2)(a).

[21] DORA, Article 5(2).

4: Governance

c) Define roles and responsibilities for ICT-related functions, and governance to oversee how those functions interact.
d) Be responsible for setting and approving the digital operational resilience strategy.
e) Approve, oversee and review the ICT business continuity policy and ICT response and recovery plans.
f) Approve and review the ICT internal audit programme, and changes to it.
g) Allocate and review the budget for digital operational resilience.
h) Approve and review policies on use of third-party ICT services.
i) Establish reporting channels relating to third-party ICT services, changes to ICT service providers, and the impact of these changes on critical or important functions.

Given the authority necessary for these duties, clearly the management body must have at least one member at the C-suite level. After all, it is unlikely some decisions can be made at a lower level – top-level policies, for instance, should have the approval of the organisation's top management or board. Furthermore, it is valuable to have someone at the top of the organisation involved so that the case for resources can be made more forcefully and to streamline communication channels.

However, it is also sensible to have elements of tactical or operational interest, which helps embed governance.

4: Governance

Tactical or operational managers can present the case for practicality to the management body, while simultaneously demonstrating their support – and comprehension – to those who will need to implement compliance measures.

This combination of perspectives will also aid in managing reporting channels. While Article 5 only refers to reporting up to the board or top management, DORA essentially relies upon effective reporting from the coalface all the way up. Providing a management body that bridges the gap between the leadership and operational concerns minimises the risk that communication channels are disrupted or ignored.

Of course, many organisations are more complex than a simple board at the top with management below and operations beneath that. As such, the management body must understand where it is appropriate to report.

As DORA is fundamentally about risk management, it would be sensible for reports to be given to the organisation's risk committee or equivalent body. In smaller organisations, this role might be fulfilled by a single director on the board, while larger organisations will have a dedicated committee at a very senior level. The management body must have access to this person or function, and it must be a two-way street.

In particular, DORA requires corporate-level reporting on the use of third-party ICT services so that the management body can remain appropriately informed. This communication channel will draw information from a number of areas within the organisation, distil it and pass it up to the board or equivalent. The fact that this is picked out as a distinct reporting channel demonstrates the

4: Governance

importance that DORA places on managing third-party risk.

This is backed up by the requirement to establish a role to monitor third-party ICT services.[22] It would be sensible for this role to be included within the management body that oversees DORA compliance. This ensures that the management body is directly involved in this process, which is clearly an excellent way to maintain oversight.

Finally, the management body needs to *"actively keep up to date with sufficient knowledge and skills to understand and assess ICT risk and its impact on the operations of the financial entity"*.[23] While the knowledge that the management body needs may differ from that needed by other staff, it is sensible to use the same processes. As most organisations will have some process for training and building skills, which will usually be well understood, it is logical to simply follow that process for whatever other skills may be needed.

Maintain the management body's knowledge may also link to the information sharing arrangements set out in Chapter VI of the Regulation, which we will go into in more detail later in this book.

---

[22] DORA, Article 5(3).

[23] DORA, Article 5(4).

4: Governance

Terms of reference

To set boundaries on the management body and protect it from being overextended, you should define some formal terms of reference.

Terms of reference outline the project's fundamental objectives, scope and guidelines. They establish the boundaries and limitations to clearly define the project's purpose and expected outcomes, which is essential in managing expectations and preventing scope creep. They also establish a shared understanding for stakeholders so that everyone involved can identify their roles and responsibilities.

Terms of reference can also be a critical communication tool, as they allow different groups or functions to understand how they fit into the project. In essence, they act as a strategic compass to minimise misunderstanding and encouraging engagement.

The terms of reference should also define project timelines, resource requirements and budget limitations. This information fosters better decision-making and helps manage project constraints.

While much of this sounds similar to the project mandate, this document should be focused on the management body and its duties, not the implementation project. This means that there will be differing levels of detail and different focuses.

At a minimum, the terms of reference should set out the following:

- **Purpose**

4: Governance

For DORA, this is likely to set out the management body's role in overseeing the risk management framework and acting as a conduit for reporting to the board.

- **Responsibilities**
  This should set out the key specific responsibilities held by the management body. As noted previously, this may include oversight of third-party ICT services in addition to the other duties required by the Regulation.

- **Commitment to cyber security risk management and digital operational resilience**
  This is essentially a mission statement for the management body. It should make it clear to each member that they are responsible for cyber security risk management and digital operational resilience.

- **DORA requirements (high level)**
  These requirements would be the five 'pillars': risk management framework, incident response and reporting, digital operational resilience testing, third-party ICT risk management, and information and intelligence sharing. These should be included as a sort of 'short-hand' reference to the management body's primary duties.

- **Participation**
  This section should describe the membership of the group; this may include a set of criteria, which would be valuable if a member leaves or otherwise needs to

be replaced. In general, this section is likely to name the key roles – chairperson, secretary, etc. – and any specific roles assigned to members. It should also define quorum, which may vary depending on the types of decisions the body needs to make.

- **Meetings**

    The management body needs to clearly set out how and when it convenes. If there are exceptions or triggers for meeting (such as following incidents, or upon significant changes in infrastructure), these should also be spelled out clearly. The key is to ensure there is a set of criteria setting out when meetings are to take place. Meetings should obviously be minuted, so there is a record of what was discussed and what decisions were made.

When meetings take place, the management body should have a standard agenda, with some flexibility for responding to immediate and new concerns. Many features of the agenda will be common, while others will necessarily be specific to DORA compliance:

- Status and actions from previous meetings.
- Changes to requirements, such as amendments in the law or guidance from ESAs/competent authorities.
- Review of changes to the framework since previous meeting.
- Monitoring and measurements, including KPIs and KRIs.
- Feedback from stakeholders.

4: Governance

- Risk and risk treatment status, covering both internal risks and supply chain risks.
- Incident reporting.
- Digital operational resilience testing.
- ICT third parties.
- Information sharing activities.
- Project updates.
- Policy changes.
- Continual improvement.
- Outcomes of audits and reviews.
- Any other business.

With the terms of reference and agenda defined, the management body will be in a good position to be able to practise and provide evidence of good governance. The latter is crucial, of course – when the competent authority comes looking for someone to blame for a perhaps inevitable failure of resilience, you will want to be able to show that you did everything reasonable to protect the organisation, its systems and its data.

CHAPTER 5: RISK MANAGEMENT

The finance sector is no stranger to risk management. It is a key skillset for nearly every organisation in the industry and well represented at board level. As such, developing a risk management framework for digital operational resilience should be a relatively trivial matter. The key issue is more likely to be developing the skills and knowledge to properly assess digital operational resilience risks, which are likely to be different from those examined in other areas of the business.

Adding to this difficulty is that the organisation must address risk management both internally and externally. This may involve not only managing contractual issues with suppliers but also requiring specialist knowledge to ensure all relevant risks are addressed by each party. In Cloud environments, for instance, there can be complex arrangements in which each party holds some responsibility.

Before getting too bogged down in the details of what could be necessary for your risk management framework, it is worth bearing in mind two key allowances that DORA sets out: the proportionality principle and the simplified framework.

The proportionality principle

The proportionality principle is a key feature that applies broadly to the organisation's risk management framework, and to the other requirements set out in Chapters III, IV and

5: Risk management

V of the Regulation where permitted. It states that the organisation *"shall implement the rules laid down in Chapter II in accordance with the principle of proportionality, taking into account their size and overall risk profile, and the nature, scale and complexity of their services, activities and operations"*.[24]

This means that the organisation has some degree of leeway in how it identifies and addresses risks to digital operational resilience. It could be very easy to find yourself overwhelmed with the scale of some risks or to find the Regulation stifling, but this provision allows the organisation to continue to act in its best interests, even where the risk could be (relatively) considerable. This is analogous to the return on investment that most risk management regimes apply – where a risk could have a significant impact but is relatively unlikely, it is not good business sense to spend a great deal combatting it.

However, this is not carte blanche to ignore DORA's requirements or to treat digital operational risks with lip service. The Regulation also directs competent authorities to consider how this principle has been applied when reviewing the consistency of an organisation's risk management framework.[25]

A robust risk assessment is critical. The organisation may make decisions about how to identify and respond to risks in alignment with its position, but it must follow a clearly defined approach that does not simply handwave things

---

[24] DORA, Article 4(1).

[25] DORA, Article 4(3).

5: Risk management

away. It is sensible to document a clear justification for your risk appetite, and to define how resilience measures are selected. If you are in any doubt about how you plan to apply the proportionality principle, it is sensible to discuss it with your competent authority.

Exemptions and the simplified framework

As previously noted, DORA provides exemptions for many organisations in specific areas. The most notable exemption is applied to *"small and non-interconnected investment firms, payment institutions exempted pursuant to Directive (EU) 2015/2366; institutions exempted pursuant to Directive 2013/36/EU in respect of which Member States have decided not to apply the option referred to in Article 2(4) of this Regulation; electronic money institutions exempted pursuant to Directive 2009/110/EC; and small institutions for occupational retirement provision".*[26] Organisations covered by this stipulation may instead opt to apply a simplified ICT risk management framework, which is set out in Article 16.

Under this framework, the organisation is still expected to achieve the same results as non-exempted organisations, but you are free to adopt whatever approach is most appropriate for your organisation. This means that you must still:

- Implement and maintain a documented risk management framework, including the mechanisms and measures necessary to manage identified risks;

---

[26] DORA, Article 16(1).

5: Risk management

- Continuously monitor ICT security;
- Minimise the impact of ICT risk by using up-to-date and resilient systems, protocols and tools;
- Quickly identify and detect ICT risks and anomalies, and handle ICT-related incidents;
- Identify key dependencies on ICT third-party service providers;
- Ensure continuity of critical and important functions;
- Regularly test controls and incident response plans; and
- Implement lessons learned following ICT-related incidents.

All of these should be pursued through documented information security and continuity processes, which allow you to demonstrate to the competent authority that you are meeting your obligations under DORA. So, while the simplified framework offers some respite from the full requirements of the Regulation, you are still expected to apply a rigorous risk management process.

Risk management framework

First and foremost, your risk management framework must be led by the digital operational resilience strategy defined by the management group, as described in the previous chapter. This strategy must define the methods to address ICT risk and achieve ICT objectives. This document essentially frames the risk management activity.

As such, it may be useful for the strategy to address this in the same phases as the Regulation. That is:

5: Risk management

- Identification
- Protection and prevention
- Detection
- Response and recovery
- Backup and restoration
- Learning and evolving
- Communication

In practical terms, however, you are likely to consider the latter half of the list as part of the response and recovery phase.

The organisation is also required to use ICT systems, protocols and tools to address and manage risks to digital operational resilience. This essentially means that the organisation cannot rely solely on management practices or the skills and knowledge of employees. You must ensure that your measures address the technological challenges.

Identification

The identification phase is what comprises the risk assessment and risk management decisions.

DORA requires the organisation to continuously identify its functions, assets and third-party dependencies, as well as the risks to those. The specific requirement essentially

5: Risk management

describes a mapping exercise with annual reviews.[27] The upside of this is that, if you have not conducted one before, it can be a good way of identifying inefficiencies and other areas where your efforts can be streamlined.

The mapping exercise starts by identifying and classifying what it is that you need to protect and then branching out to determine dependencies. For instance, a function relies on information, systems, personnel and potentially third-party service providers. Each of these is a potential point of failure or a target for attack.

Ensuring you map the relationships and dependencies between each element is critical. This enables you to more accurately describe how they might be interrupted – which is to say, how they might be subject to risk.

ISO 27001 provides a clear process for conducting information security risk assessments, which can be applied to this part of the risk management framework. It essentially follows the same pattern:

1. Establish criteria for conducting risk assessments and quantifying risks (defined by your digital operational resilience strategy).

---

[27] DORA, Article 8(1): *"As part of the ICT risk management framework referred to in Article 6(1), financial entities shall identify, classify and adequately document all ICT supported business functions, roles and responsibilities, the information assets and ICT assets supporting those functions, and their roles and dependencies in relation to ICT risk. Financial entities shall review as needed, and at least yearly, the adequacy of this classification and of any relevant documentation."*

5: Risk management

2. Identify what you need to protect.
3. Identify risks.
4. Assess the consequences and likelihood of those risks.
5. Evaluate the risks for treatment.

This article also requires you to perform a risk assessment *"upon each major change in the network and information system infrastructure, in the processes or procedures affecting their ICT supported business functions, information assets or ICT assets"*.[28] This can be built into your change management processes relatively simply and helps the organisation stay on top of risk without needing to conduct full-scale risk assessments more frequently than necessary.

Obviously, for all of these processes to function properly, you must review the results periodically – it is no good having a control in place that takes up resources if it is not effective. Part of this involves reviewing and maintaining your inventories and the overall mapping.

Protection and prevention

The protection and prevention phase addresses the organisation's need to continuously protect and monitor its important and critical functions. Many activities in this phase will have been identified as controls to minimise risk in the identification phase.

All the activities in this phase need to achieve some key objectives for DORA compliance:

---

[28] DORA, Article 8(3).

5: Risk management

- Secure the means of data transfer.
- Minimise the risks to confidentiality, integrity, availability and authenticity to information and ICT systems, including technical flaws.
- Protect data from risks associated with data management, including human error.

There are two primary requirements in this phase: to continuously monitor and control ICT systems and tools; and to define and document ICT security policies, procedures and tools.

Monitoring involves regularly inspecting the activity and effectiveness of the organisation's systems and its resilience measures. Inspecting the activity is important as it will often provide the first indication of issues that could lead to interruptions or failures of resilience. Inspecting the effectiveness is also important because it provides confidence that your measures are working or will be effective when an incident occurs.

Depending on how these measures function, monitoring can be manual or automated, which should be identified when you select and design the measures in the previous phase. Selecting a control is not as simple as just indicating something that you would like to do – it also means planning what it needs to achieve, how it will be implemented, how it will be checked and how to assess its efficacy.

When defining your policies, procedures and tools, you should consider how best to design resilience into the organisation. Your policy, for instance, can require that all new systems consider resilience at the design stage, which

5: Risk management

may reduce the costs and other overheads involved in securing the systems.

Developing effective policies is a fine art. All too many are buried in complex language and obscure grammar, when policies should be readily understood by all who need to operate under them. For instance, if you ask your employees to sign a document saying they have read and understood the information security policy, this only says that someone has signed something – it does not mean that they can apply what it says. Policies dictate the parameters for managing certain activities, so they are essential when new events or activities arise: they provide guidance on how to approach the situation and good practice until a documented process can be produced.

Having a strong set of policies has a trickle-down effect. Processes and procedures that implement the policies must fall in line with the rules and objectives established in the policies, leading to more secure and resilient network infrastructure, stronger authentication and identity management, and so on. DORA establishes key areas that policies (and the resulting procedures and tools) should address in Article 9(4).

Detection

DORA requires financial entities to implement mechanisms to detect anomalous activities and to identify potential material single points of failure. Detecting anomalies, such as events and incidents, as soon as possible is crucial to minimising the impact and improving the speed at which the organisation can recover to business as usual.

5: Risk management

Detection monitoring is a crucial activity that can take place in real time and in retrospect, and using both automated and manual tools. For most purposes, however, real-time, automated tools are likely to be the most valuable. For instance, security information and event management (SIEM) tools are capable of inspecting information gathered as data moves through digital environments and alerting personnel when anomalies are detected. These tools provide a valuable source of information not only about the existence of a threat but also its specific activities, which can make isolating, neutralising and recovering from the threat considerably easier.

Of course, it is no good having detection measures if they do not work or if there is no one available to act on the alerts. To ensure this is the case, DORA requires the organisation to regularly test its detection measures, which should include ensuring that someone is properly alerted and able to act on the information. This means linking these measures to your incident response processes.

Building layers of detection measures is a sensible approach because of the many ways a disruption can occur. With overlapping detection using differing but related metrics, you can also build resilience into your framework. This helps ensure that anomalies are detected and may also provide additional data points to better understand the nature of the event.

The most significant challenge in implementing such measures will be determining what to monitor and what to look for. Some elements of this will be resolved through the risk assessment, while others can be informed by threat

5: Risk management

intelligence, and information from your competent authority and similar agencies.

Response and recovery

As mentioned previously, it is easy to view this element of the risk management framework as encompassing all the remaining elements. This means viewing backup and restoration, lessons learned, and communication as part of your response and recovery processes.

The overall process should aim to ensure that your critical and important functions are protected and can continue to operate (although potentially with some limitations), that the incident is contained or isolated, and that the organisation recovers quickly to full functionality. Not all elements will contribute directly to all parts of the process. Backups, for instance, are a valuable tool and essential when there is data loss.

While ISO 27001 offers an excellent basis for the information security aspects of your risk management framework, it is relatively light on detail for incident response and – in particular – business continuity. For that reason, we recommend looking at ISO 22301, which focuses on business continuity. Many organisations will already have some elements of continuity in place, and it will often be based on ISO 22301, so it may be a simple matter of adapting those processes to take digital operational resilience into account.

For smaller organisations or those with less experience in the area, ISO 22301 offers an excellent approach that integrates well with ISO 27001.

5: Risk management

First and foremost, this phase demands that you have an ICT business continuity policy, which is put into effect through defined incident response processes and business continuity plans. Your ICT continuity policy should be aligned with – or even part of – your wider corporate business continuity policy. This will ensure that your work addresses the organisation's important and critical functions.

Your policy and the resulting processes and plans must be documented and accessible. Accessibility is often overlooked, but for incident response and continuity purposes, it is essential. After all, if the plans are stored on the company fileserver but the fileserver is down, then they are not much practical use.

Any effective approach to business continuity must be based on a realistic assessment of the risks and an understanding of the relative impact of different events on the organisation's various functions. Part of this is encapsulated in the risk assessment, but a further step is necessary: business impact analysis (BIA).

A BIA is particularly valuable for your business continuity plans because it enables you to appropriately prioritise functions for recovery. This means that you can minimise overall disruption by targeting problems that cause the greatest harm – whether that be through direct loss of revenue or through knock-on impacts on other business functions.

The policy and plans should also set out how communications are managed through disruptions. This usually means appointing a key role to oversee communications in line with a prescribed process for

5: Risk management

communicating internally and externally about the incident. Because this may involve communicating with authorities, the key role should have the authority to secure whatever information the authorities need, and to make decisions about when to communicate with customers and other third parties, and to what level of detail.

As the adage goes, 'No plan survives contact with the enemy', and the same is true of your incident response and business continuity plans. As such, it is essential to test your plans at least annually and after any significant changes to ICT systems that support important or critical functions.

DORA notes that tests should especially focus on outsourced functions and arrangements.[29] Testing is not necessarily a full simulation and can be handled in a number of ways, including tabletop exercises and limited-scope tests – the real key output is to make sure that all the people involved know their parts, and to find any aspects of the plans that fail or are weak and can be amended through reviews.

DORA also requires the organisation to retain records of activities before and during disruptions. This means that your incident response and business continuity plans need to produce evidence of your processes in action. These records may need to be submitted to the competent authority, but – more usefully – they can also be fed into your lessons learned processes to improve the effectiveness of your responses.

---

[29] DORA, Article 11(4).

CHAPTER 6: INCIDENT RESPONSE AND REPORTING

It feels rather odd for DORA to separate out incident response and reporting from the risk management framework when a distinct part of that framework is describing how the organisation should respond to incidents. It is telling that much of this part of the Regulation is directed at the competent authorities and ESAs: it is addressing how an incident can affect the sector, not just the organisation itself.

It is useful to know how the competent authorities will receive and react to incident reports, of course, but it is not essential for compliance with the Regulation.

For financial entities, the key requirements revolve around the incident management process, classification of incidents and cyber threats, and reporting of incidents and threats. While most of this chapter in the Regulation addresses incident response, it is important not to neglect threats. The Regulation encourages organisations to report significant threats, which enables competent authorities to spread key information and minimise the risk posed by those threats.

While response and recovery are partially addressed in the previous chapter as part of the risk management framework, this part of the Regulation looks at the larger framework for incident management. Many elements of the work done in the risk management framework will effectively be enacted through this incident management

6: Incident response and reporting

process – the risk assessment identifies the incident response measures and the incident management process puts those into action.

There are a number of ways to ensure your incident management meets DORA's requirements, as the Regulation is not terribly prescriptive. In general, however, the best-practice approach will involve several key parties and processes. These should all be established under a central incident management policy. Many organisations will already have an equivalent document, and it should not need much amendment to apply to incidents that could affect digital operations.

The organisation should also establish an incident response team and an incident review board. The response team should have defined roles and responsibilities that align with the skills and experience necessary to respond to incidents. This might include technical experts, communication specialists and legal/compliance staff.

The incident response team will, obviously, need to be prepared to respond. This means that they must be given appropriate training and the opportunity to test their skills. This can be partially incorporated into the necessary testing of incident response and business continuity plans.

The review board, meanwhile, is likely to be much the same as the management body for the risk management framework. There is no need to create a separate oversight entity for this. Their duty will be to assess the handling of major incidents and provide recommendations for improvements.

6: Incident response and reporting

The incident management process will pass through several phases:

1. Incident detection and early warning
2. Incident reporting and logging
3. Incident classification and prioritisation
4. Incident response
5. Communication and notification
6. Recovery and documentation
7. Root-cause analysis
8. Continual improvement

This broadly aligns with many of the stages set out in best-practice guides such as the CREST Incident Response model, so it is equally valid to simply take those models and apply them to your own organisation.

Incident detection and early warning systems should be identified during the risk assessment. This is because they will be best placed at the sites with the greatest risk or the greatest exposure. For instance, intrusion detection systems on the network perimeter. It is also important to remember that detection and early warning does not just include automated systems or devices: threat intelligence can provide early clues about a cyber attack or the characteristics of new threats, which can then be fed into detection systems. Logs can be analysed after the fact to detect incidents that are not identified as they break in, and so on. And staff, of course, should be trained to report events that could constitute incidents, such as strange behaviour from systems, sudden increases in phishing emails, and so on.

6: Incident response and reporting

When an incident – or an anomaly that *could* be an incident – has been identified, it needs to be reported and logged. This can be automated through SIEMs and intrusion detection systems, or manually in the case of human detection. The key factor is to ensure that the appropriate parties – the incident response team – know that an incident may have occurred. Logging the incident allows the organisation to keep track of it as it progresses, including the actions taken to contain and mitigate it, and to resolve and recover. In its simplest form, the log should record the date and time of the incident, a description, impact assessment and actions taken.

The incident response team then needs to classify the incident and prioritise the response. This is the crux of digital operational resilience: correctly assessing how best to maintain operations while resolving the incident. The classification should aim to identify what (systems, functions, information, etc.) the incident is affecting and their criticality for operations.

DORA mandates using the following as part of the classification[30]:

- Number or relevance of clients/counterparts affected, and the number of transactions affected, and whether the incident has reputational impact.
- Duration, including service downtime.
- Geographical spread.

---

[30] DORA, Article 18(1).

6: Incident response and reporting

- Impact on confidentiality, integrity, availability and authenticity.
- Criticality of services affected.
- Economic impact, both direct and indirect.

These criteria will be expanded on through technical standards yet to be developed by the ESAs.

It is likely that much of this information is not available when the response needs to go into action, and the organisation will collate more and more as the incident develops and the organisation responds. The final result of this classification should be included in reporting about the incident.

Classification will lean heavily on the business impact assessments conducted previously. In an ideal world, the incident will align with one of the business continuity plans, enabling the incident response team to quickly deploy the appropriate measures exactly as planned. The real world, of course, is not so convenient, and it is likely the team will need to make decisions on the fly to best preserve the organisation's ability to operate.

Something that is easily forgotten in the heat of the moment is compliance. Having criminal hackers at the door does not mean that you can ignore the law. You must still meet your legal, regulatory and contractual obligations. Given the nature of the industry, much of this is likely to fall under the various financial regulations and the GDPR or other data protection laws. These are all likely to have key requirements around incident response and reporting – in particular, the GDPR has specific requirements for

6: Incident response and reporting

reporting breaches of personal data, and failure to comply with this law can magnify your problems.

All the way through the process, you will need to communicate – whether internally or with external parties. Internal communications are likely to be essential for resolving the incident, while external communications are more likely to be necessary for compliance purposes.

What might be overlooked, however, is ensuring that you have multiple ways of communicating. If an incident takes down your email servers, for instance, do you have other methods of passing information through the incident response team? How can you validate that alternative communications are secure and coming from the right people? Do you have someone appointed to manage external communications and the means to give them the information they need?

Part of this includes reporting on the incident to management. While it may not be necessary to provide blow-by-blow details as and when they happen, the incident response team will need to provide clear information about the incident and its handling intermittently during the incident and when the incident has been resolved, as this information will then be fed into any report to the competent authority.

When reporting incidents and significant threats to the competent authority, the stated aim of the Regulation is to use a harmonised reporting form or template.[31] This will ensure that all organisations are able to provide the

---

[31] DORA, Article 20.

6: Incident response and reporting

information that the competent authorities need, and can prepare, knowing what information will be asked of them. Until these templates are ready, however, best practice would be to ask your competent authority about the information they will need about incidents and significant threats.

DORA requires financial entities to notify the competent authority at a number of stages throughout the incident's life cycle[32]:

- An initial notification, which will likely be unable to provide any significant amount of information about the incident.
- An intermediate report *"as soon as the status of the original incident has changed significantly or the handling of the major ICT-related incident has changed based on new information available"*. This should be followed by updates when relevant changes occur or when requested by the competent authority.
- A final report when root-cause analysis has been completed, even if there is ongoing mitigation and recovery.

When entering the recovery phase of the incident response, documentation is extremely important. Recording how you go about remediating issues and returning services and functions to business as usual – and the effects of those actions – will enable you to improve your incident response

---

[32] DORA, Article 19(4)(b).

6: Incident response and reporting

in future. For instance, it may be possible to start recovery sooner, to do things more efficiently or more effectively, or to take specific actions that reduce the likelihood that the incident will reoccur.

With services and functions restored, the root-cause analysis should be conducted to identify precisely how the incident occurred. This may be a simple process or it could involve more aggressive measures, including digital forensics and criminal investigations.

As an incident is a risk become manifest, the organisation should aim to identify the threat and the vulnerability that, together, allowed it to occur. If this risk was already identified by the risk assessment and under treatment, the organisation then needs to examine the effectiveness of its measures.

Risk management is, as previously noted, governed by making reasonable decisions about the cost of treatment, so it is possible that nothing went wrong – it was simply the odds against you in this case. However, the analysis may also turn up other ways to react to the risk that could be more effective without incurring a significant increase in resource costs. Equally, it could identify a risk that had not been identified during the risk assessment.

Based on the results of the root-cause analysis and other data produced during the incident and the response, the organisation should aim to improve its digital operational resilience. Using the data they have gathered, the incident response team, the review board and the management team should examine ways to improve security, reducing vulnerabilities and exposure, and streamline the response for the future. Depending on the severity of the incident,

6: Incident response and reporting

the competent authority may also advise or mandate key changes to the risk management framework and/or the incident management process.

CHAPTER 7: DIGITAL OPERATIONAL RESILIENCE TESTING

A sensible element of any information security and resilience programme is testing. After all, if you are simply relying on your security measures and responses to work, you are putting a lot of faith in the fairly abstract risk assessment processes that you use to pick them.

Testing the security and resilience measures is crucial to ensure the effectiveness of the defence mechanisms against potential threats, and to identify where vulnerabilities may still exist or are under-protected. Such testing helps identify and rectify weaknesses in the system before malicious actors exploit them or accidents expose them. Regular testing provides insights into potential entry points for cyber attacks, allowing the organisation to fortify its defences and stay ahead of evolving threats.

Testing is not just about your defences, however: it contributes to your overall resilience. By subjecting security measures to simulated attacks, you can evaluate how well they can withstand and recover from a security breach, which can inform your incident response and business continuity plans. This proactive approach can help minimise downtime and damage in the event of a real incident.

Furthermore, the continual evolution of technology and cyber threats demands regular testing to ensure that security measures remain up to date and aligned to modern

7: Digital operational resilience testing

needs. This adaptability is crucial for staying ahead of emerging threats and maintaining a robust security posture.

This means that testing should not simply be a process of checking that your measures are in place and doing what you *expect* them to do. You must ensure that those measures are addressing the real risks and concerns, and that you will be able to effectively respond to incidents, even those you do not necessarily expect. It is a process of testing your fixed defences and your adaptability.

DORA essentially sets out two levels of testing: testing of ICT tools and systems, and advanced testing based on threat-led penetration testing. These describe very different practices.

The Regulation mandates annual testing, specifically using a *"range of assessments, tests, methodologies, practices and tools"*.[33] It does not specify what these should be, however – the organisation needs to determine for itself what it needs to do to properly assess its defences and resilience measures. This multifaceted approach ensures that each measure or defence is assessed according to its design – simply checking logs, for instance, is not going to highlight weaknesses across the board. Equally, a full-strength penetration test would be excessive for many systems, especially isolated internal systems that are unlikely to be exposed to criminal hackers.

For this reason, the Regulation states that testing should follow a risk-based approach that recognises the

---

[33] DORA, Article 24(2).

7: Digital operational resilience testing

organisation's specific environment, threats and needs.[34] Once again, this is also affected by the proportionality principle: while DORA may appear to mandate expensive and time-consuming processes, these should be applied according to the nature, scale and complexity of your organisation's operations.

One of the key elements of testing is independence. When testing anything – as we should all know – it is important not to test your own work. The Regulation takes this principle into account[35]; however, this could be difficult for smaller organisations. The level of independence necessary may be difficult to achieve. As such, it may be useful to identify automated testing methods and tools, which can take an objective look at your defences and other measures. Beyond this, carefully designed testing scenarios and methods, or external parties, may be necessary to ensure that testing is conducted thoroughly, appropriately and independently. It is not clear whether the proportionality principle can exempt the organisation from ensuring the independence of testing.

Whether issues are identified, DORA states that the organisation must have *"procedures and policies to prioritise, classify and remedy all issues [...] and shall establish internal validation methodologies to ascertain that all identified weaknesses, deficiencies or gaps are fully addressed"*.[36] This means that the organisation must have a

---

[34] DORA, Article 24(3).

[35] DORA, Article 24(4).

[36] DORA, Article 24(5).

7: Digital operational resilience testing

clear, systematic method; it should not be based on kneejerk reactions, or haphazardly assigning resources based on loud voices or gut feelings.

Testing of ICT tools and systems

DORA does not set out terribly detailed requirements of this type of testing; it relies on the organisation to identify what tools and systems it needs to test, and the appropriate ways of testing those tools and systems.

Obviously, to do so in accordance with the Regulation, you must be able to identify all of your *"ICT tools and systems"*. There is no immediate definition for these, but Articles 24 and 25 make it clear that this should address ICT assets that relate to your services, important and critical functions, and security and resilience measures. This is a broad requirement, but the interconnected nature of ICT networks and systems means that many elements can be tested simultaneously using the same methods. For instance, by conducting load testing on a web application, you are simultaneously assessing the load capacity for the underlying infrastructure.

The organisation should be identifying what needs to be tested through its risk management framework, and in determining security and resilience measures identifying how they can be tested. As mentioned previously, ISO 27001 can streamline a lot of this: testing of controls and other processes will be an inherent part of your information security management system.

DORA lists a number of types of testing, but they are not mandatory, nor is it a comprehensive list. The key is to match the testing to the function. For instance, vulnerability

7: Digital operational resilience testing

scans can quickly and cheaply assess your network boundaries for common vulnerabilities; a more involved penetration test may only be necessary for web applications or interfaces with other organisations; a gap analysis can provide a good overview of your security against a defined standard.

Not all types of testing are simple or can be done in-house, even by large organisations. Some testing requires specific technical skills or technologies. Much like achieving independence in testing, you may find it necessary to use third parties. One of the key benefits of this is that your contracts provide some protection in the event of a failure that should have been identified in testing. While the competent authority may have something to say about your choice of third party, it will act as a factor in your favour to demonstrate that you recognise your organisation's limitations and make a good-faith effort to conduct appropriate testing.

As noted previously, testing should be at least annual, but may be more frequent depending on the tool or system, or on the basis of risk assessment. Furthermore, changes in networks, other infrastructure or the threat environment may make it sensible to conduct testing more frequently, even when a fresh risk assessment may not be necessary.

Threat-led penetration testing

Threat-led penetration testing (TLPT) is a very involved process. It is much more complex and thorough than most other penetration testing, and often results in a months-long engagement with highly specialised third parties.

7: Digital operational resilience testing

On the plus side, not every organisation will be required to submit to TLPT. Under the Regulation, the competent authorities are responsible for identifying the organisations that must perform the testing.[37] Under the terms of this stipulation, the competent authorities will take the proportionality principle into account, which means it is unlikely that any organisation required to take the testing will be able to argue against the competent authority. So, if your competent authority says you have to do it, you do not have much wiggle room to get out of it.

On a positive note, TLPT is only required every three years. Given how involved the testing can be, this is reasonable. On the one hand, if it was more frequent, the organisation would spend an inordinate amount of time doing little else. On the other hand, the thoroughness of the testing means that it serves as an excellent way of preparing for the most severe cyber threats, and measures implemented to respond to any identified weaknesses should be capable of protecting the system from any but the direst threats.

DORA does not provide a specific definition for TLPT, but most competent authorities or EU member states already have definitions that can be applied. While not a member of the European Union, the UK's Bank of England, for instance, has defined the CBEST (Critical National Infrastructure Banking Supervision and Evaluation

---

[37] DORA, Article 26(8).

7: Digital operational resilience testing

Testing) framework, which is likely to be similar to those established within the EU.[38]

The CBEST model has four phases:

1. Initiation
2. Threat intelligence
3. Penetration testing
4. Closure

The initiation phase covers all the activity leading up to the test itself: notification that the financial entity must conduct TLPT, scoping the testing and identifying/procuring the resources necessary to complete the testing. The scope will be critical: because TLPT can be relatively intrusive and expensive, it is important to ensure that the scope is as tight as it can be. It would also be sensible to have the scope reviewed and approved by the competent authority to avoid having to repeat the exercise later.

The threat intelligence phase comprises the planning of the testing activity. This involves identifying the key functions and services within the scope of the testing, the relevant threats and their capabilities, the scenarios to be used in testing, validation of the planning (by the competent authority or similar entity), and assessing the organisation's ability to collate and understand threat intelligence. This is assessed separately from the rest of the testing because it is entirely possible that poor intelligence has still led to

---

[38] *https://www.bankofengland.co.uk/financial-stability/operational-resilience-of-the-financial-sector/cbest-threat-intelligence-led-assessments-implementation-guide.*

7: Digital operational resilience testing

effective defences, but it indicates that the organisation may not be fully equipped to respond to new threats.

The penetration testing phase is, as you might expect, when the meat of the testing occurs. It encompasses constructing the detailed testing plans, executing the tests, assessing the organisation's detection and response capabilities, and reviewing the results of the test. While this sounds relatively straightforward, it is important to remember that the testers will be executing attacks as if they were highly motivated, experienced and skilled attackers – it is not the same as a vulnerability scan or an opportunistic attack. Under CBEST, this test must also be conducted against live production systems and environments unless there are legal or ethical constraints. This can be highly disruptive, so the organisation must be sure it is ready – such testing is not something to go into blind!

The final phase – closure – contains the follow-up actions from the testing. This includes developing a remediation plan, debriefing the organisation and stakeholders on the results, and actions from the competent authority. A final element within this is the competent authority's analysis of TLPT results more generally, which may result in additional regulation within its sphere of interest. Remediation plans will need to be approved by the competent authority and should address all identified issues that present a notable risk.

As you can see, this is potentially a long and intrusive process, and can represent a significant expense.

7: Digital operational resilience testing

The testing itself can be conducted by internal resources provided they meet certain criteria.[39] In particular – and what are likely to be the main blocks on using internal resources for most organisations – the testers must have a high level of skill in penetration testing and threat intelligence, and must be *"certified by an accreditation body in a Member State or adhere to formal codes of conduct or ethical frameworks"*.[40] Few organisations are likely to have people with such skills and certifications on staff, so finding a suitable set of testers is almost certain to involve outsourcing.

A final key thing to consider when preparing for TLPT is how to minimise the impact of the testing on the organisation more widely. Given the nature of the testing, there is the risk of significant impacts within the scope of the project, but the organisation needs to be prepared to be able to manage the rest of its resilience activities without distraction – it would, after all, be a painful lesson to be vulnerable to real attackers in one area while ethical hackers are probing another!

---

[39] DORA, Article 27.

[40] DORA, Article 27(1)(c).

CHAPTER 8: ICT THIRD-PARTY RISK MANAGEMENT

Third parties obviously present a significant risk to any organisation. Suppliers and service providers make things simpler for most organisations, but you must, by default, put a lot of faith in contracts to ensure that they meet their security and resilience obligations.

Some of the largest data breaches in history were caused by exploiting third parties. The Target breach of 2013 is probably the most notable. In that incident, a refrigeration contractor with access to Target's internal systems was first breached by the attackers, who used the supplier's access to move into Target's systems.[41] From this humble beginning, the attackers were able to access sensitive payment card data, customer personal information and other data. The final toll resulted in 40 million stolen credit and debit card records and 70 million customer records, an $18.5 million settlement, and immeasurable reputational damage.[42]

---

[41] Michael Kassner, "Anatomy of the Target data breach: Missed opportunities and lessons learned", ZDNET, February 2015, *https://www.zdnet.com/article/anatomy-of-the-target-data-breach-missed-opportunities-and-lessons-learned/*.

[42] Corrin Jones, "Warnings (& lessons) of the 2013 Target data breach", Red River, October 2021, *https://redriver.com/security/target-data-breach*.

8: ICT third-party risk management

Of course, you might consider that Target is a retail brand that exists in a different threat environment and uses different suppliers – how relatable is this scenario? Sadly, the scenario is potentially worse for organisations in the financial sector because ICT suppliers can have a staggering impact on operations. Furthermore, an attack that does not gain access to information can still cause a significant disruption to critical and important functions. Remember: DORA is not a strictly cyber security law, it is about operational resilience.

So, the next question might be why this is addressed separately from the risk management framework established earlier. After all, this is simply another risk management exercise. The answer is held in the recitals. For instance, Recital 9 notes that Union harmonisation in monitoring ICT third-party risk has been absent, and so it is necessary to highlight this in the new law. This is expanded on in Recital 29:

> *"In the absence of clear and bespoke Union standards applying to the contractual arrangements concluded with ICT third-party service providers, the external source of ICT risk is not comprehensively addressed. Consequently, it is necessary to set out certain key principles to guide financial entities' management of ICT third-party risk, which are of particular importance when financial entities resort to ICT third-party service providers to support their critical or important functions."*

DORA addresses ICT third-party risk as a separate concern because, in the past, it has not been well handled, nor has there been strong oversight. Given the risk posed by third

8: ICT third-party risk management

parties, as noted by the ESRB in Recital 3, it is important to ensure that the Regulation addresses this clearly.

Furthermore, while ICT third-party suppliers are identified as 'financial entities' in Article 2, the actual ICT supply chain can be incredibly deep, and some organisations that provide ICT services may not be readily identified or themselves recognise their involvement. Because of this, organisations need rigorous processes to ensure that security and resilience requirements are propagated all the way down the supply chain.

DORA addresses ICT third-party risk in two parts: requirements for use of third parties and requirements for oversight.

Requirements for use of third parties

DORA establishes two key principles for managing ICT third-party risk. The first principle states that financial entities remain responsible for their obligations under the Regulation; there is no way to contract out of this. While your service providers may absolve you of having to implement specific measures, you remain responsible for ensuring that they have done so. The second principle simply restates the proportionality principle, clarifying how it applies in relation to ICT third-party services and contracts.

Coming out of these principles are a number of specific requirements that build on the risk management framework to ensure that third-party services are appropriately managed.

8: ICT third-party risk management

ICT third-party risk strategy

The Regulation requires a strategy for managing ICT third-party risk. This essentially requires a framework for managing ICT risk as a subset of the organisation's main risk management framework. It is helpful to think of it in these terms because it encourages you to address third-party risk as a separate type of risk and not something that can necessarily be addressed in the same way you respond to other risks.

The strategy needs to take the organisation's multi-vendor strategy into account and include a policy on the use of services to provide critical or important functions. As such, it forms the crux of the organisation's approach to using ICT third-party services.

The multi-vendor strategy is initially raised in Article 6 of the Regulation as part of the risk management framework. The purpose of the strategy is to identify the organisation's key dependencies and to set out the organisation's rationale for the specific mix of services that it uses. It does not need to place significant limits on the use of ICT third-party providers; rather, it needs to set out how the organisation determines when a third-party service is necessary or acceptable. As a strategy, it should be linked to the organisation's business objectives.

The policy on the use of services in critical or important functions should be much more prescriptive. Like any policy, it should set out rules and objectives, which means it needs to provide clear conditions on the use of services in these cases. Outsourcing critical and important functions – or elements of those functions – presents a potentially heightened risk to the organisation because it, obviously,

8: ICT third-party risk management

removes the organisation from many of the decisions about how to secure and assure the critical and important functions. While contracts put legal weight behind the organisation's needs, they are not a magic bullet. As noted previously: you cannot contract out of responsibility for your organisation's digital operation resilience.

Your ICT third-party risk strategy – and the elements related to it – need to be reviewed with some regularity by the management body. Where there are objectives and KPIs, these should therefore be provided for the review. Where any incidents have occurred in relation to third parties, these also need to be taken into account.

Register of ICT third-party services

In addition to the strategy and its constituent parts, the organisation is required to create and maintain a register containing information about all ICT third-party services.[43] This register needs to record the key information about the services and contracts to deliver those services, and it needs to be in a format that can be presented to your competent authority.

This latter point is important because the Regulation specifically requires the organisation to report to the competent authority on several key elements. These elements include the following:

1. The number of new third-party arrangements for ICT services.

---

[43] DORA, Article 28(3).

8: ICT third-party risk management

2. The types of contractual arrangements.
3. The ICT services and functions being provided.

Furthermore, the competent authority may ask to see the organisation's register of ICT third-party services. As such, the register needs to be capable of being easily queried to provide the information necessary for reporting to the competent authority, but also needs to be digestible by the competent authority directly. Providing a register that the competent authority cannot easily understand or requires excessive extra detail to make sense of is simply likely to result in enforcement action.

Finally, the organisation needs to report to the competent authority "in a timely manner" when it intends to use ICT third-party services to support its critical or important functions. This also applies when an existing function becomes critical or important. This highlights the need to have an effective inventory of functions alongside their classifications, and which can be reconciled against the register of ICT third-party services.

Contractual requirements

Obviously, contracts are an essential part of arrangements between your organisation and its service providers. Contract law is well understood and should not need much of a primer here, but there are several aspects of contracts that DORA expresses an interest in.

When establishing contracts, financial entities must look into the nature of the service and the service provider. There are several specific activities that the organisation must do as part of this: due diligence and risk assessment, ensure audit and inspection are addressed within the contract,

8: ICT third-party risk management

ensure there are clear service termination provisions, and have documented exit strategies.

Due diligence and risk assessment before engaging a service provider should be second nature to any organisation in the financial sector. Much of this will be focused on assessing the degree to which the service provider meets DORA's requirements and other financial regulations, and the position it may leave the organisation in if the service is disrupted.

The organisation should also establish how the service provider will demonstrate compliance with contractual terms. Usually, this is through audits and inspections, which may involve a third party to protect both parties and their intellectual property. If the organisation chooses to conduct the audits itself, it needs to be sure that its auditors have the technical knowledge to properly assess the service provider.

Termination clauses in contracts need to address how the contract can be ended before completion – usually due to failure to meet contractual terms, security failures, etc. DORA specifically notes that the organisation should be able to terminate a contract if any of the following conditions are met[44]:

- The ICT third-party service provider breaches applicable laws, regulations or contractual terms.
- Circumstances occur that are capable of altering the performance of services. For instance, the service

---

[44] DORA, Article 28(7).

8: ICT third-party risk management

provider is no longer able to provide necessary bandwidth, changes in the law prohibit the service provider from performing certain activities, etc.
- The service provider fails to adequately address risks, in particular risks to the confidentiality, integrity, availability and/or authenticity of data.
- When the competent authority can no longer supervise the organisation due to the contract. For instance, where the service cannot be adequately assessed by the competent authority due to being hosted in a hostile state.

The organisation needs to back this up with exit strategies designed to minimise disruptions and maintain compliance with DORA and other legal or regulatory requirements. While this is a useful thing to prepare for all notable service providers, DORA specifically states that this is necessary for services that support critical or important functions. These strategies need to be maintained, because the obvious necessity when exiting a contract is securing replacement services to compensate as quickly as possible, and ideally without loss of service quality.

These exit strategies should address conditions beyond those presented in termination clauses. After all, contracts sometimes come to an end for more benign reasons – replacement of service providers with cheaper or more reliable alternatives, bringing services in-house, and so on. In fact, this is one of the key points that the Regulation makes about the risk assessment: identifying suppliers that are not easily replaceable. As part of the risk assessment

8: ICT third-party risk management

before engaging a service provider, you should identify fallback options and other alternatives.

The specifics of the contract are addressed in Article 30 of the Regulation. This sets out the key provisions that must be covered. Many of these elements are likely already in place for almost any service contract, so updating template contracts and the procurement process should be a relatively easy process. Amending existing contracts to take these additional points into account may be slightly more problematic, but amending contracts partway through is not a new process for any business.

Information security standards for service providers

As noted early in DORA, the Regulation does not just apply to financial entities: it also sets out requirements for the ICT third-party service providers that work with them. In this instance, these requirements are established by requiring the financial entity to set minimum standards.

The first requirement is that ICT third-party service providers must comply with *"appropriate information security standards"*.[45] Where the services relate to critical or important functions, the financial entity has to take into account whether those standards are the most up to date and highest quality. There are many standards that a service provider might align with – obviously, beginning with ISO 27001.

ISO 27001 may also be supported by a range of supplemental standards, such as ISO 27017 (code of

---

[45] DROA, Article 28(5).

8: ICT third-party risk management

practice for information security for Cloud services), ISO 27018 (protecting personal data in the Cloud), ISO 27701 (personal information management), and so on. The particular mix of standards will be determined by the nature of the services on offer and the organisation's level of interest in security.

Other relevant standards and frameworks might include:

- **NIST SP 800-171**
  NIST's more comprehensive special publication, 800-53, features several hundred controls, which is likely to be overwhelming for many organisations. NIST SP 800-171 is an abbreviated selection of those controls, aiming to provide strong information security with only 110 controls.

- **NIST Cybersecurity Framework**
  This is a relatively simple – but flexible – framework for managing cyber security and incident management. It includes processes for improving the maturity of security measures over time.

- **COBIT**
  COBIT operates as a governance framework for IT, which enables the organisation to align its security objectives with wider organisational objectives.

- **CIS 18**
  The Center for Internet Security has maintained a list of what it considers the most important security controls for a number of years, and in the current iteration describes 18 controls. Each of these sets out

8: ICT third-party risk management

a number of safeguards, arranged into implementation groups.
- **Cyber Essentials Plus (in the UK)**
  Cyber Essentials is a government scheme in the UK to ensure organisations apply a minimum standard of cyber security. While the basic level offers some assurance of security, Cyber Essentials Plus backs this up with audited evidence that the controls are in place.

ISO 22301 may also be valuable. While it is not an information security standard, it does provide excellent guidance on business continuity, which obviously translates well into digital operational resilience. As such, you could consider it a further benefit offered by the service provider.

It is also important to understand the degree to which a service provider has aligned to the security standards that it claims. Accredited certification is the only way to be certain that the organisation has not only implemented the standard correctly but is also engaged in an ongoing process to maintain the effectiveness of its security measures. However, it is worth noting that not all standards have an associated certification scheme, so asking a provider for proof of their compliance with the NIST Cybersecurity Framework, for instance, is likely to result in a discussion about audits and assurance rather than a simple certificate demonstrating compliance.

Concentration risk

'Concentration risk' describes the risk presented by using a single supplier for too many operations, relying on a single

8: ICT third-party risk management

service that could have significant knock-on effects if it ceases or is unavailable, and relationships between suppliers and sub-contractors that could cause disruptions. It is about putting too many eggs in one basket.

Initially – and when later looking into using third parties – the organisation must identify single points of failure (SPOFs). These are the locations – either physical or logical – where things can fall down, causing a wider disruption and potentially threatening digital operational resilience.

The Regulation focuses on two areas of concentration risk in Article 29. The first of these examines the risk in relation to a single supplier – first, where they cannot be easily replaced, and second, where multiple services are provided by that supplier. In these cases, the organisation runs the risk that a failure of that one supplier could have a significant impact on operations.

The second area of concentration risk is where a supplier relies on subcontractors. This deepens the supply chain, and may mean that a single subcontractor could disrupt the service, thus introducing a number of areas where disruption could occur. The obvious solution here is to ask the primary supplier to ensure there are redundancies in place for each subcontractor, and to ask how this would work in practice. However, supply chains like this can be extremely long and involve a large number of potential points of failure – where this is the case, a different solution for the service is likely preferable.

8: ICT third-party risk management

Oversight of critical third-party service providers

Oversight of third parties by competent authorities is something that many financial organisations will not need to worry about, with one exception: lead overseers.

Lead overseers are individual entities that are assigned to oversee critical third-party service providers. This is likely to apply to organisations like Amazon, Microsoft, and so on – organisations that provide major infrastructure or other services to a large cross-section of the financial sector.

The lead overseer's primary duty is to assess the service provider's security and resilience measures, which ensures that these core service providers are able to properly serve clients across the financial sector. In essence, this is likely to serve as centralised assurance that these service providers are unlikely to be the source of any major disruption, even taking into account concentration risk. This does not absolve the financial entity of doing its own due diligence and risk management, but it should provide a compelling set of evidence.

CHAPTER 9: INFORMATION AND INTELLIGENCE SHARING

The final core chapter of DORA is less about protecting the organisation than it is about protecting the wider industry. No organisation exists in a vacuum, and while some organisations may be rivals, there is much to be said in favour of sharing threat information and cyber intelligence – even with rivals.

Of course, given the interaction between many organisations in the financial sector, protecting your compatriots is *also* another way of protecting yourself. After all, if a partner organisation is compromised, the attackers may be able to glean information that can be used to target your organisation. By drawing from a pool of information, all parties are better able to secure themselves.

The Regulation itself does not have much to say about this – it is a single article overall and simply sets out a few parameters for sharing information. This is a sensible approach, as the law does not obligate organisations to take part, and imposing excessive rules would simply discourage organisations from sharing information and, therefore, reduce the amount of threat intelligence available within the sector.

Essentially, DORA allows financial entities to exchange cyber threat information and intelligence between themselves as long as they meet specific criteria in doing so. Primarily, the information must be shared securely so

9: Information and intelligence sharing

that it protects business confidentiality and complies with the GDPR.

The Regulation even points out the sorts of information that may be useful to share: *"indicators of compromise, tactics, techniques, and procedures, cyber security alerts and configuration tools"*.[46] However, there is no limit to the types of information that might be usefully shared, so it is best to consider sharing information based on its content rather than its format. This sort of information can provide a valuable heads-up for other organisations in similar situations.

Where organisations choose to share information under this article, DORA requires that there be formal arrangements covering elements such as how public authorities and service providers are involved, and the use of specific technologies or platforms for sharing information. These arrangements should be documented and agreed between all parties.

Finally, the Regulation requires organisations involved in such information-sharing arrangements to notify their competent authority. Notifications must be made when joining and when leaving such information-sharing groups.

---

[46] DORA, Article 45(1).

FURTHER READING

IT Governance Publishing (ITGP) is the world's leading publisher for governance and compliance. Our industry-leading pocket guides, books and training resources are written by real-world practitioners and thought leaders. They are used globally by audiences of all levels, from students to C-suite executives.

Our high-quality publications cover all IT governance, risk and compliance frameworks and are available in a range of formats. This ensures our customers can access the information they need in the way they need it.

Other resources include:

- CyberComply: CyberComply makes compliance with cyber security requirements and data privacy laws simple and affordable, *www.itgovernance.co.uk/shop/product/cybercomply*
- *The Cyber Security Handbook – Prepare for, respond to and recover from cyber attacks* by Alan Calder, *www.itgovernance.co.uk/shop/product/the-cyber-security-handbook-prepare-for-respond-to-and-recover-from-cyber-attacks*
- *IT Governance – An international guide to data security and ISO 27001/ISO 27002, Eighth edition* by Alan Calder and Steve Watkins, *https://www.itgovernance.co.uk/shop/product/it-*

Further reading

governance-an-international-guide-to-data-security-and-iso-27001iso-27002-eighth-edition

For more information on ITGP and branded publishing services, and to view our full list of publications, visit *www.itgovernancepublishing.co.uk*.

To receive regular updates from ITGP, including information on new publications in your area(s) of interest, sign up for our newsletter at *www.itgovernancepublishing.co.uk/topic/newsletter*.

Branded publishing

Through our branded publishing service, you can customise ITGP publications with your company's branding.

Find out more at

www.itgovernancepublishing.co.uk/topic/branded-publishing-services.

Related services

ITGP is part of GRC International Group, which offers a comprehensive range of complementary products and services to help organisations meet their objectives.

For a full range of resources on DORA visit *www.itgovernance.co.uk/shop/category/dora*.

Training services

The IT Governance training programme is built on our extensive practical experience designing and implementing

Further reading

management systems based on ISO standards, best practice and regulations.

Our courses help attendees develop practical skills and comply with contractual and regulatory requirements. They also support career development via recognised qualifications.

Learn more about our training courses and view the full course catalogue at *www.itgovernance.co.uk/training*.

Professional services and consultancy

We are a leading global consultancy of IT governance, risk management and compliance solutions. We advise businesses around the world on their most critical issues and present cost-saving and risk-reducing solutions based on international best practice and frameworks.

We offer a wide range of delivery methods to suit all budgets, timescales and preferred project approaches.

Find out how our consultancy services can help your organisation at *www.itgovernance.co.uk/consulting*.

Industry news

Want to stay up to date with the latest developments and resources in the IT governance and compliance market? Subscribe to our Security Spotlight newsletter and we will send you mobile-friendly emails with fresh news and features about your preferred areas of interest, as well as unmissable offers and free resources to help you successfully start your projects. *www.itgovernance.co.uk/security-spotlight-newsletter*.

Milton Keynes UK
Ingram Content Group UK Ltd.
UKHW020302130624
443828UK00010B/39